REDRAWING *the* MAP

The Partition of Ireland

CATHLEEN SMALL

Cavendish
Square

New York

Published in 2019 by Cavendish Square Publishing, LLC
243 5th Avenue, Suite 136, New York, NY 10016

Copyright © 2019 by Cavendish Square Publishing, LLC

First Edition

This publication represents the opinions and views of the author based on his or her personal
experience, knowledge, and research. The information in this book serves as a general
guide only. The author and publisher have used their best efforts in preparing this book and
disclaim liability rising directly or indirectly from the use and application of this book.

All websites were available and accurate when this book was sent to press.

Library of Congress Cataloging-in-Publication Data

Names: Small, Cathleen.
Title: The partition of Ireland / Cathleen Small.
Description: New York : Cavendish Square, 2019. | Series: Redrawing the map | Includes glossary and index.
Identifiers: ISBN 9781502635648 (pbk.) | ISBN 9781502635624
(library bound) | ISBN 9781502635631 (ebook)
Subjects: LCSH: Ireland--Juvenile literature. | Ireland--History--Juvenile literature.
Classification: LCC DA906.S58 2019 | DDC 941.5--dc23

Editorial Director: David McNamara
Editor: Erin L. McCoy
Copy Editor: Michele Suchomel-Casey
Associate Art Director: Amy Greenan
Designer: Jessica Nevins
Production Coordinator: Karol Szymczuk
Photo Research: J8 Media

CONTENTS

CHAPTER ONE

The Irish Partition in a Nutshell

A single island off the west coast of England, Scotland, and Wales is today split into two states: an independent nation called Ireland and a six-county region called Northern Ireland, which is part of the United Kingdom. These territories weren't always separate, however. In fact, this island was independent of all of its neighboring countries from prehistoric times until the mid-twelfth century. During that time, it had a completely separate social, political, and cultural order, commonly referred to today as Gaelic Ireland. How it came to be divided in two is a centuries-long story of religious conflict and political power struggles, beginning when the first outsiders came ashore on the coast of the Emerald Isle.

Opposite: Danish Vikings were among the first people to attack the island of Ireland early in its history in the hopes of conquest.

Early Ireland

The peoples of Gaelic Ireland were divided into clans ruled by kings or chiefs. These clans sometimes warred between themselves, but Gaelic Ireland remained a territory independent of foreign sovereignty for centuries.

Clans generally relied on agriculture, especially raising livestock, for their survival. The predominant religions were polytheistic or pagan, though Christianity eventually became the island's dominant religion. Citizens of Gaelic Ireland developed common styles of dance, art, sport, music, dress, and architecture that are recognized today as reminders of Ireland's rich culture.

However, the Norman invasion of 1169 CE marked the beginning of the end for Ireland as an independent nation. From that point forward, conflict with neighboring countries mounted as different factions struggled for control over the island.

Outsiders had visited Gaelic Ireland before—the Vikings, for instance, first arrived in the ninth century. The Vikings intermarried with Irish citizens, and a new group known as Norse-Gaels emerged. The Norse-Gaels mostly assimilated to Gaelic culture and

A RELIGION OF THE NATURAL WORLD

The pagan Gaelic Irish believed in multiple gods and goddesses, and they also believed that spirits were contained in all aspects of the natural world, including animals, plants, bodies of water, weather, and even rocks.

eventually became almost indistinguishable from native Gaels.

Other outsiders, though, were more determined to take control of Ireland. The French, the Spanish, the Scottish, the Welsh, and especially the English—all these nations had an interest, at one time or another, in ruling Ireland.

The struggle for control was long and tumultuous; the Gaels weren't about to give up their country without a fight. Wars intervened, temporarily distracting England from its interest in taking over Ireland, and famine and disease wracked the island, as well. For hundreds of years, control over Ireland, and the dominance of different cultural and religious factions, would remain in the balance, shifting again and again.

During the same period, England and other European countries were facing religious upheaval. The sixteenth century brought about the Protestant Reformation, a direct challenge to the Catholic Church, which had been Europe's most formidable and authoritative religious institution for more than a millennium. Protestant groups such as Lutherans and Calvinists formed churches and began to spread across Europe, and the Church of England officially split from the Catholic Church under the rule of Henry VIII in the 1530s. The split led to two distinct and powerful religious groups that would come to define—and divide—Ireland: Catholics and Protestants.

A Border Drawn Largely by Religion

This religious division eventually became a decisive factor in the partition of Ireland. Calvinists from Scotland had crossed the Irish Sea and settled in northern Ireland, particularly in the Ulster region; as a result, these counties had a relatively large population of Protestants. In the south of Ireland, however, Catholics remained in the majority.

By the early eighteenth century, Protestant England controlled Ireland, and as a result, Protestants enjoyed economic and political privileges. This drove a rift between Catholics and their English rulers. In the nineteenth century, when England attempted to establish self-governance in Ireland, many citizens in southern Ireland were in favor of the idea, but Protestants in the north generally opposed it. This created a division between republicans, who wanted Ireland to have its own government independent of the United Kingdom's, and unionists, who wanted Ireland to remain a part of the UK.

This division was contentious, and, following a series of brutal skirmishes and rebellions, the Irish War of Independence broke out. With the aim of preventing further violence, the Government of Ireland Act 1920 partitioned the country into two parts: a much larger southern region called Ireland (sometimes referred to as the Republic of Ireland), made up of twenty-six counties, and a smaller northern region, officially known as Northern Ireland and made up of six

Ireland, often called the Republic of Ireland, is geographically much larger than Northern Ireland.

counties. Today, Northern Ireland is part of the United Kingdom, and Ireland is a sovereign state with its own parliamentary government.

The partition of Ireland was the result of centuries of religious and political upheaval. Today's borders were drawn by thousands of conflicts, large and small, and countless important figures, famed and forgotten. Understanding Ireland as it is now requires traveling back in time, long before the island was divided in two.

CHAPTER TWO

Ireland Before Borders

Ireland's history before it was partitioned into two regions is long and contentious. Most of the conflicts centered on the religious divide between Protestants and Catholics, as well as questions of sovereignty— should Ireland be self-governing or should it be governed by England and the United Kingdom?

Nearly eight hundred years of conflict laid the groundwork for the partition of Ireland in 1921. To understand all the factors that contributed to the split, it's best to start all the way back with the Normans.

The Normans in Ireland

The Normans were originally Vikings from Scandinavia who had since migrated to Normandy, France— hence their name. In 1169 CE, the year the initial

The Battle of Hastings, fought in 1066, was one of many skirmishes during the Norman invasion.

Norman invasion took place, Gaelic Ireland was divided into kingdoms, each of which was ruled by a high king. Dermot MacMurragh, former king of Leinster, had been deposed in 1167, and now he sought the Normans' help in reclaiming his rule. The Normans were indeed successful in gaining control over Leinster—but then they began to raid other Irish kingdoms with the permission of both the pope and King Henry II of England.

Henry II hoped to conquer Ireland in the name of England, and in many ways, he succeeded. He named his son, John—who later ascended to the English throne—lord of Ireland, and together, he and the Normans set out to conquer Ireland.

The Norman invasion lasted for years as, in collaboration with England, they gained more and more control over the island. This systematic encroachment would come to define the next eight hundred years of Irish history, over the course of which Ireland would be in a continuous state of unrest, the central conflict being whether the island should fall under English (later British) rule or be self-governed.

In theory, the English succeeded in taking over Ireland during the Norman invasion. However, in practice, the transfer of power didn't go so smoothly. English monarchs typically resided in England, and the

THE LEGEND OF ROBIN HOOD

Under King John's rule, Ireland was run by a series of sheriffs who would collect fines and taxes and enforce Norman Common Law. Robin Hood, the mythical outlaw in England who would steal from the rich and give to the poor, was reacting to King John's structure of fee-collecting sheriffs.

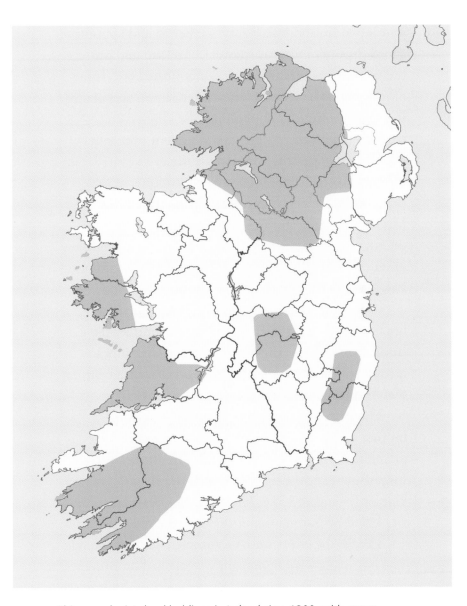

This map depicts land holdings in Ireland circa 1300, with green territories held by native Irish and cream-colored areas held by Normans.

journey to Ireland wasn't easy, so they would appoint a lord deputy or viceroy to oversee Ireland and protect the monarchy's interests there. As it turned out, some of the lord deputies were more intent upon augmenting their own power than upholding the king's—and without the monarch's direct and present oversight, many were successful in doing just that.

The Normans never completely conquered the entire island. They tended to live in Leinster and Munster counties in the south. Many Normans eventually assimilated to Irish culture and life, and they often observed Irish law rather than English Common Law because the penalties were less strict.

In the mid-thirteenth century, the Gaelic Irish began to fight back in an attempt to reconquer their lands. Interestingly, they used Norman weapons and tactics, and by the beginning of the fourteenth century, they had regained a fair amount of territory.

The Irish decided to ally with Edward Bruce, brother of the king of Scotland, to lead a charge to drive the Normans out of Ireland. They were nearly successful—so close, in fact, that Edward was crowned king of Ireland in 1316. However, two years later, he was killed by Normans and the recovery stalled.

The Gaelic effort wasn't a complete failure, though. The Normans were significantly weakened by Bruce's campaign, and they were finally driven out of Ulster, which would later become a significant region in the partition of Ireland.

The Normans now turned to the English for help. In response, King Richard II traveled to Ireland in 1394 with ten thousand troops. He was the first English monarch to set foot on Irish soil in nearly two centuries, but within a year, he had gained control of a number of Irish territories, each of whose Gaelic chieftains submitted to English rule.

These new allegiances were not to last. The English monarch still found it difficult to govern the island from across the Irish Sea, and tensions erupted in Ireland yet again. For more than three centuries, no English monarch visited Ireland, and the battle for control raged on.

English Religion and Politics

Events that didn't even take place on Irish soil—including religious conflicts and power struggles within the English monarchy—affected Ireland. While it may have been difficult for people to cross the channel between England and Ireland, such conflicts crossed over relatively easily.

The Wars of the Roses

Such was the case with the Wars of the Roses, a series of battles for control of the English monarchy, fought between the Houses of Lancaster and York. Richard, the Duke of York, was named heir to the British throne in 1447, and that same year he was named viceroy to

The Wars of the Roses spanned three decades and were fought by those who supported the House of Lancaster versus those who supported the House of York. Ultimately, the House of Lancaster prevailed.

Ireland. The Irish pledged loyalty to Richard of York and even went so far as to say that English writs were invalid. It was thought that the Irish used the unrest in England to declare their own autonomy.

The House of York gained control of the monarchy for a time, before the throne returned to the House of Lancaster in 1485. However, Lancastrian king Henry VII left a Yorkist, the Earl of Kildare, in charge of Ireland. It was a recipe for unrest.

King Henry VII watched the situation in Ireland unfold for nearly a decade before finally replacing Lord Deputy Kildare with a Lancastrian lord deputy, Sir Edward Poynings. The king hoped Poynings could regain English control in Ireland.

The new lord deputy enacted Poynings' Law, which stated that the Irish Parliament could convene only upon approval from England and that the only laws it could pass were those approved by England. Poynings' Law stayed on the books for nearly three hundred years.

The Reign of Henry VIII

Henry VIII may be England's most notorious king, given his penchant for beheading people (including some of his wives). However, he was also a noteworthy figure in Irish history. Under previous English rule, the earls of Kildare had been allowed to hold a fair amount of power in Ireland. Henry, however, was a more insecure and suspicious ruler, and he wanted to limit the Kildares' influence in Ireland.

King Henry VIII was responsible for the Church of England's split with the Catholic Church. This portrait of the king was painted by Hans Holbein the Younger, a German and Swiss artist known for his portraiture.

Aside from his personal brutality, Henry VIII is known for introducing the Protestant Reformation in England. This religious movement had been sweeping across Europe, challenging the Catholic Church and gaining more and more followers. When Henry's first wife, Catherine of Aragon, failed to produce a son and heir to the throne, the Catholic pope refused to grant Henry's request for an annulment—so he turned to Protestantism instead.

Henry initiated what came to be known as the English Reformation. Other theological and political disputes factored into the reformation, but the primary impetus was Henry's desire for an annulment. The 1534 Act of Supremacy installed Henry as the Supreme Head on Earth of the Church of England, which effectively brought England under Protestant rule.

Because the Irish Parliament was effectively controlled by the English Parliament, it came as no surprise that the former passed the same law in 1536, establishing the Church of Ireland under the leadership of the reigning monarch of England. From this moment on, power struggles, rebellions, wars, and the eventual partition of Ireland would hinge, in large part, on an unremitting conflict between Catholics and Protestants on the Emerald Isle.

In 1541, the Irish Parliament took yet another step toward unification with England by declaring Henry VIII the king of Ireland. As harsh a ruler as Henry was, his policy for Ireland was relatively nonviolent. He established a system of surrender and regrant in Ireland, which meant that if an Irish chieftain submitted to English rule, he would be "regranted" a title of nobility. Rather than conquering kingdoms by force, Henry attempted to win local leaders over by granting them titles.

The New English in Ireland

After King Henry VIII's death in 1547, his nine-year-old son, Edward VI, was crowned king. Edward never reached adulthood, so although he was technically king, the country was ruled by a Regency Council.

Administrators from the Regency Council attempted to continue Henry's policy of surrender and regrant, and establish other policies that would strengthen England's hold on Ireland. These administrators became known as the New English, as opposed to the Old English, who had settled in Ireland as far back as the Norman invasion. The New English were seen to be more directly tied to the Crown.

One policy the New English put forth was the establishment of plantations, which took land from the native Irish and gave it to English settlers. Sometimes the Irish who remained stayed on as workers, but they no longer owned their land—they were just tenants.

A Return to Catholicism

When Edward VI died at the age of fifteen, Mary I, a Catholic, ascended to the throne. However, she ruled for only five years before she died and was replaced by her Protestant half sister, Elizabeth I.

In 1570 Pope Pius V declared Elizabeth I a heretic and excommunicated her, nominally releasing her subjects from obeying her and opening the door for Catholics in Ireland to freely practice their own religion. Many of the Old English living in Ireland at the time were Catholic, so this action pleased them. However, it made the English monarchy suspicious of their loyalty to the Crown—if they were *really* loyal, the monarchy felt, they would be willing to live under the Church of England. Eventually, the monarchy began to view these Old English Catholics as more aligned with the Gaelic Irish and began treating them as such.

Questions of religious freedom in the region had practical impacts, even affecting policy and trade. Catholics had strong trading links with much of Catholic Europe, which Protestants felt weakened their own trading position. The religion people chose to practice had far-reaching effects on their daily lives.

Rebellion, Religion, and Landownership

Battles for control and disputes over what system of law and religious doctrine would command the island led to a series of wars and rebellions on Irish soil, including the Nine Years' War (1593–1603), which left Ireland, at last, completely under British rule. By 1688, after another spate of violent conflicts, Protestantism had finally deposed Catholicism as the official religion of the English Crown. However, even in the face of

After Elizabeth I was excommunicated, the Catholic Irish and Old English had some hope that Catholicism would regain footing in Ireland. Numerous Catholic rebels operated in the country, but their attempts at revolt were often small and unsuccessful.

One rebel, however, started a movement that had more traction. James Fitzmaurice Fitzgerald led the Desmond Rebellions in Munster starting in 1569. He and his fellow rebels were quickly

Life on Munster Plantation was more difficult than the English had anticipated, thanks in part to the land being very difficult to farm.

stopped and by 1573 had accepted pardons from Elizabeth I. Fitzgerald, however, continued his attempts at insurrection. In 1575, he traveled to France and Spain to seek assistance in his goal of liberating Ireland, and he returned in 1579 with a small army supplied by the pope himself and prepared to fight a holy war.

Fitzgerald was killed, but some of the Old English, including the Earl of Desmond, continued the fight. The clashes lasted another four years before, at last, the English triumphed. Because

English law established that lands owned by rebels should be forfeited to the Crown, the English took control of Munster (about half a million acres, or 202,000 hectares) and established the Munster Plantation. The property was to be farmed using English methods and settled by the English. All the native Irish were to be removed from the land, with defensive measures established to keep them out.

Munster Plantation was doomed from the start. Much of the land the English had seized was very difficult to farm, so the English settlers had to keep the native Irish close at hand to help them cultivate it. In 1598, as part of the Nine Years' War, hostile natives struck back and destroyed the plantation. Once again, a lack of oversight had crippled English efforts on Irish soil.

these English victories, disputes over landownership continued, fueled by rival claims and struggles for doctrinal and political dominance.

The Plantation of Ulster as a Line of Defense

When the Irish lost their last outpost, a Gaelic kingdom called Tyrone, at the end of the Nine Years' War, the English began to make plans for another plantation like the Munster Plantation, one that would encompass Tyrone and five other counties in Ulster, in the far northern reaches of Ireland.

The Plantation of Ulster suffered from a similar setback to that which Munster faced: the land was reportedly dangerous, so the gentlemen, former soldiers, government officials, and so-called "deserving Irish" that the English hoped would populate the plantation proved difficult to attract. Thus, as with Munster, native Irish were permitted to stay on the land, even though they didn't own it anymore.

Ulster was more successful than Munster, however. Within thirty years, it had been settled by more than forty thousand people, a third of whom were deemed capable of carrying weapons, according to the English. This was noteworthy from a defensive standpoint: one of the reasons the Munster Plantation fell was that they didn't have strong enough defenses to fight off rebel attackers. Ulster had enough weapon-carrying residents to effectively deflect enemies.

The Plantation of Ulster's presence in the north would eventually be a decisive factor in the partitioning of Ireland. Areas around the development would become more industrialized than the south of Ireland as a result of the plantation's success, which would solidify the region's reliance on trade with Britain, a relationship they would later be loath to give up.

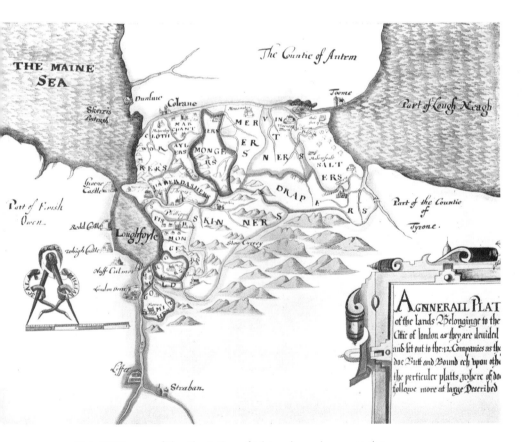

This 1622 map of the Plantation of Ulster shows how vast the plantation once was, spanning much of what is now Northern Ireland.

Charles I and Thomas Wentworth

When James I died in 1625, he was succeeded to the throne by his son, Charles I. Unrest was taking over Ireland again—this time because the Old English feared they were losing their political power there. The Irish Parliament was increasingly controlled by Protestants, and the Old English also weren't benefitting from the plantations put in place by the English, who offered incentives to New English supporters of the Crown, but not necessarily to those who had been settled in Ireland for generations.

Charles I faced the problem of not having enough money to maintain his army, so he didn't want to alienate the Old English, who tended to be wealthy. Charles's solution was to appoint Thomas Wentworth as lord deputy of Ireland. Wentworth was eager to help raise money for Charles by imposing fines on the undertakers at plantations. The undertakers could be fined for anything from taking over church lands to employing native Irish on the plantation. The plan worked, and the money came in quickly.

Needless to say, the fined citizens weren't fond of this plan, and Wentworth made even more enemies when he tried to impose the Episcopal religion on those Presbyterians who had settled in the region. Both Presbyterians and Episcopalians were technically part of churches derived from Protestantism, but they were in essence two separate churches with different practices and policies, and people weren't keen on being forced to change their church affiliation.

The common disgust for Wentworth as lord deputy served as a uniting factor for the Old English and New English in Ireland, and they worked together to have him impeached and put to death in 1641. However, their alliance was only temporary, and once Wentworth was gone, they once again divided back into two separate camps.

The Irish Rebellion of 1641

Sixteen years into the reign of Charles I, the king's conflicts with the English Parliament and unpopular policies in Ireland were inciting a state of chaos. Irish rebels saw this as an opportune time to try to win back control of their nation.

The native Irish who had been working on the Plantation of Ulster staged a revolt. The rebels made it clear that their quarrel was with the English Parliament, not with the king. This was an important distinction. It led Parliament to believe that the rebels were aligned with King Charles I, which ultimately sparked the English Civil War.

In Ireland, the violent fighting in and around Ulster lasted for several months. It's thought that at least four thousand Protestants were killed in the attacks, and many Catholics were killed as the Protestants struck back.

Among the atrocities committed during the Irish Rebellion of 1641, Irish Catholics reportedly drowned English Protestants.

As the conflict spread, the Old English formed an alliance with the rebels. In the summer of 1642, this alliance resulted in the establishment of the Confederation of Kilkenny, which was made up of Irish Catholic nobles, military leaders, and clergy members.

It was designed to administer the Catholic parts of Ireland with a parliament, a supreme council, and a military, and it was loyal to Charles I.

While Protestants faithful to England controlled parts of Ulster, Munster, and Leinster, Catholics governed a large segment of Ireland after the confederation was established. However, dissension among the ranks would spell the demise of the confederation just seven years later. Old English members were happy to declare their loyalty to Charles I, but they wanted to keep their land and wanted the right to religious freedom. The Gaelic Irish, for their part, wanted a return to the system of ruling Gaelic chieftains. Conflicting goals prevented long-term alliances from taking root.

The Cromwellian Conquest of Ireland

In 1649, the English Parliament ordered the execution of Charles I. A split in the legislative body had led to the formation of a so-called Rump Parliament. It lasted from 1649 to 1653, during which period military leader Oliver Cromwell emerged as a powerful political force. In 1649, Cromwell arrived in Ireland as commander in chief and lord lieutenant, accompanied by an army of thousands.

Cromwell was determined to reestablish English rule, avenge the Irish Rebellion, and implement the Adventurers Act of 1642, which gave land confiscated from rebels to people who contributed money to the effort to defeat the Irish rebels.

Cromwell and his army of twelve thousand were wildly successful in their efforts. Their first endeavor was a brutal invasion of Drogheda, near Ulster—a bloody battle that Cromwell's army easily won. Over the ensuing months, Cromwell and his forces moved through the province of Munster; many Catholic lives were lost along the way.

Cromwell's efforts lasted for four years, and by May of 1653, the last of Catholic Ireland had been defeated. The native Irish population dropped drastically during Cromwell's stay, in part due to his brutal invasions, but also as a result of widespread famine and an outbreak of the bubonic plague. It was, without a doubt, a dark time in Irish history.

After 1653, the English government began to take land away from anyone who had opposed Parliament, including both the Gaelic Irish and the Old English. The land was mostly seized from Catholics, while Protestants who had opposed Parliament were typically only charged heavy fines. The property was then redistributed to English settlers.

This process was an attempt to populate the land with the loyal English and rid it of the Irish—a form of ethnic cleansing. It wasn't entirely successful, though. As had happened in earlier eras, the land-owning English often ended up intermarrying with the native Irish, and many Catholics retained their faith despite the persecution they faced.

Charles II and the Act of Settlement

When Cromwell died in 1658 and Charles II took the throne in 1660, policies of landownership in Ireland shifted yet again. Charles II was loyal to the Irish who had been loyal to his father, Charles I—but he didn't want to upset Parliament. His compromise, in the end, was the passage of the Act of Settlement in 1662, which stated that anyone who could prove that they were innocent of involvement in the Irish Rebellion could get their land back.

However, Charles II had underestimated how many Irish could prove their innocence, and there ended up being more claimants than there was available land. So, in 1665, the Act of Explanation was passed, prohibiting further claims and declaring that settlers under Cromwell must forfeit a third of their land to those Irish people who had already proved that they were innocent.

The Rise of Protestant and Parliamentary Control

When Charles II died in 1685, James II ascended to the throne. James was Catholic, but his eldest daughter and successor, Mary, was a Protestant, so Parliament assumed that a Protestant would soon rule the country once again.

What legislators didn't foresee was that James's second wife, Mary of Modena, would give birth to a son who was baptized Catholic—and who would become heir to the throne over his daughter, Mary.

The Protestant William of Orange, also known as William III, won the War of the Three Kings, claiming rule over the United Kingdom.

Leading Protestants sought to remedy this problem by creating a Bill of Rights that allowed James's initial heir, Mary, to become a joint monarch with her husband, William of Orange. In 1688, William and Mary arrived in England, and James fled to France shortly thereafter, ceding the throne and granting the majority of power to Parliament.

James's secession established two paradigms that last to this day: first, there would never be another Roman

Mary, wife of William of Orange and daughter of James II, fought for rule against her father.

Catholic monarch of the United Kingdom, which was now comprised of a unified England, Scotland, and Ireland. Second, British Parliament had become more powerful than the monarch. Today, the Crown is more of a figurehead than a ruling presence.

A Last Sally for Catholic Rule

James II did attempt to regain power. He had appointed Catholic Richard Talbot, Earl of Tyreconnell, to head up the Irish army. When James lost the throne, Talbot declared that Ireland would remain loyal to James—and he had a Catholic army behind him.

James also had French support. He was an ally of King Louis XIV of France, who supplied James with an army, and the War of the Three Kings broke out. While the battles were fought in Ireland, the conflict had ramifications throughout Europe, since William and Mary were allied with other European rulers opposed to Louis XIV.

The Battle of the Boyne was a turning point in the War of the Three Kings. Throughout much of Ireland, Catholic landowners had regained their property and no longer faced Parliament-imposed restrictions. Ulster, however, was under the control of the Williamites. In 1690, opposing forces met at the Battle of the Boyne, and it was a mismatch of power for certain—James's army had fewer than eleven thousand men, whereas William's had nearly thirty-six thousand. William's forces were victorious, James II was exiled to France, and William and Mary retained control of the throne.

The War of the Three Kings ended when the Treaty of Limerick was signed in 1691. The treaty granted Irish Catholics freedom of religion but required them to pledge allegiance to William and Mary if they were to keep their land.

It was a slippery slope, even for Catholics who did pledge their allegiance. Parliament enacted a series of penal laws that restricted Catholics from teaching or running schools, gaining education outside of Ireland, owning or using weapons, or owning a horse worth more than a small sum. These laws were a way to keep Catholics politically powerless.

In a further attempt to snuff out Catholicism in Ireland, Parliament passed the 1697 Banishment Act, which required most Catholic clergy to leave Ireland. Moreover, in 1704, the Registration Act required that each Catholic priest be registered, with no more than one per parish. The Registration Act also stated that upon a priest's death, he could not be replaced.

These efforts didn't succeed, however. Catholicism would remain very present in Ireland, and the power struggle between Catholics and Protestants would continue for centuries more—as would the struggle between English and Irish rule.

CHAPTER THREE
Geographical Influences on the Mapping of Ireland

Ireland is an island, so in one sense the border is easily defined by the Irish Sea and the Celtic Sea on the eastern edge, the North Atlantic Ocean on the western edge, and the North Channel along the northeastern edge of Northern Ireland.

However, the delineation of today's Ireland–United Kingdom border, more commonly called the Irish border, is much more complicated. The dividing line cuts a wedge out of the northeastern part of the island. That territory, referred to as Northern Ireland, is today part of the United Kingdom. The border was established as a result of a long history of religious and political struggle, but natural geographical features played a key role in defining its dimensions, as well.

Opposite: During the Troubles, the British army placed roadblocks to prevent car bombs built by the Irish Republican Army from being brought into Northern Ireland.

The Irish Countryside and the Border Region

The landscape of Ireland draws millions of visitors every year, and it has inspired many an artist to wax poetic on its rain-soaked grasslands and on the low hills and coastal highlands that surround a flat lowland at the heart of the island. Irish novelist Frank Delaney expresses an Irishman's adoration for this landscape in his 2005 book, *Ireland*:

> When I come out on the road of a morning, when I have had a night's sleep and perhaps a breakfast, and the sun lights a hill on the distance, a hill I know I shall walk across an hour or two thence, and it is green and silken to my eye, and the clouds have begun their slow, fat rolling journey across the sky, no land in the world can inspire such love in a common man.

William Butler Yeats, one of the most prominent poets in Irish history, lived through the wars and violence that plagued the late nineteenth and early twentieth centuries before partition, but while many of his poems take a sober stance on the political state of his country and commemorate such bloody events as the Easter Rising, the poet finds solace in the lakes (or *loughs*, as the Irish call them), bogs, and rivers that crisscross the Irish countryside in poems such as "The Lake Isle of Innisfree":

I will arise and go now, and go to Innisfree,
And a small cabin build there, of clay and wattles made;
Nine bean-rows will I have there, a hive for the honey-bee,
And live alone in the bee-loud glade.

And I shall have some peace there, for peace comes
     dropping slow,
Dropping from the veils of the morning to where the
     cricket sings;
There midnight's all a glimmer, and noon a purple glow,
And evening full of the linnet's wings.

These same enchanting landscapes and geographical features characterize the border between Ireland and North Ireland, though a natural belt of small, steep hills have historically made traffic between Ulster and other parts of the island difficult and may partly account for cultural differences between the two regions.

Physical Characteristics of the Border

The Irish border stretches for 310 miles (499 kilometers) from the northern edge of Ireland at the estuary of Lough Foyle (opening into the North Channel) to the northeastern fjord of Carlingford Lough (along the Irish Sea). However, the distance from Lough Foyle to Carlingford Lough as the crow flies is actually much shorter—if one were to draw a straight line between the two, it would be only about a quarter as long.

The Irish border is long and winding because it skirts the edges of the six counties of Ulster that make up Northern Ireland. As it leaves Lough Foyle in the north, it runs along the western edges of Londonderry, Tyrone, and Fermanagh counties, then turns east and follows the southern borders of Fermanagh and a bit of Tyrone, then the western and southern edges of Armagh. The other two counties in Northern Ireland—Down and Antrim—do not share any part of the border with Ireland. They are flanked by water as they jut out at the very northeastern tip of the island.

County lines often followed waterways, so the Irish border traces those same waterways through the countryside. As a result of these rivers, some parts of the border are nearly impassable except for traveling by boat or fording by foot, as is the case with some stretches of the Woodford River, which—combined with the mountains, tiny islands, and lakes around the border of Counties Fermanagh (Northern Ireland) and Cavan (Republic of Ireland)—draws a looping and winding borderline.

The Irish border would actually be much shorter if Donegal, in the northwest, were part of Northern Ireland; after all, it lies within the more heavily Protestant Ulster province, most of whose counties are to the north of the present-day border. However, County Donegal is part of the Republic of Ireland, so the border extends along its eastern edge. The resulting geographic isolation from the rest of the republic has at times earned Donegal the moniker of "the forgotten

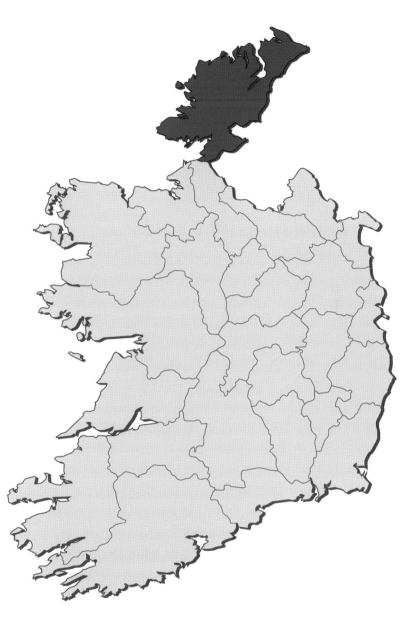

The border between County Donegal, highlighted in red, and County Leitrim just below it is quite short, although both counties are in Ireland. Both are bordered by Northern Ireland.

county," though many in Donegal prefer their former tourism tagline, "Up here it's different."

To travel between Donegal and the rest of the Republic of Ireland, there is only a narrow boundary line—6 miles (9 km) wide—between Counties Donegal and Leitrim. Therefore, it's often more direct for travelers to cross the border and pass through Northern Ireland to reach their destination.

Traveling Across the Border

There are approximately three hundred major and minor border crossings between Ireland and Northern Ireland. The exact border can even be difficult to locate at times because neither Ireland nor Northern Ireland officially marks it. Instead, drivers can usually identify which country they're in by looking at the road signs: those in Northern Ireland are generally in English and use miles as their unit of measure, whereas signs in Ireland are often in both English and Irish and use kilometers as their unit of measure.

There are also differences in how the countries mark the edges of their roads, how they name their routes, and what colors they use for their road signs. Mailboxes are often different colors, too. In Northern Ireland, they're usually red, whereas in Ireland they're generally green. Finally, Ireland uses the euro as currency, whereas Northern Ireland uses United Kingdom currency based on the British pound. Savvy travelers between the two

In Killybegs, Ireland—not far from Northern Ireland—some road signs are written in English, while others are written in both English and Irish Gaelic.

A topography of small, steep hills called the drumlin belt crosses south Ulster, dividing the region from the rest of Ireland. This terrain, sometimes likened to a "basket of eggs," proved a strategic advantage for northerners during the Nine Years' War.

In 1587, Irish Gaelic lord Hugh O'Neill became the Earl of Tyrone, a kingdom in Ulster. Under the English policy of surrender and regrant, he could surrender his lands to the English, be regranted them as the property of the Crown, and claim a title of English nobility. O'Neill was keen to do this, but he also wanted to continue to rule Tyrone in the Gaelic tradition, which was not acceptable to the monarchy. So began the Nine Years' War (1593–1603).

The battles were fought all across Ireland but were particularly concentrated in Ulster. The rough terrain in the drumlin belt reduced visibility and hindered troop movements, which O'Neill used to his benefit.

In the end, however, the English prevailed again. After a treaty failed to keep the peace, O'Neill's lands were forfeited to the Crown. Tyrone, the last Gaelic outpost, was gone, and Ireland was left completely under English rule.

Because the drumlin belt was, for so many centuries, a natural obstacle for travelers, some geographers have argued that it defined Ulster as a "natural region," relatively isolated from the rest of the island. The drumlin belt would see intense deforestation and road-building in the seventeenth and eighteenth centuries, lessening geographical obstacles even while some cultural and historical divides between north and south remained deeply rooted.

countries will notice gas prices and store signs using the appropriate currency for whichever country they're in.

The border between Northern Ireland and Ireland is open; travelers can freely pass over it without stopping at checkpoints, and no passport is needed to pass from one country to the other. When Northern Ireland experienced several decades of unrest and guerrilla war in the late twentieth century, military checkpoints were installed at major border crossings between the two nations, and minor crossings were closed. However, the last of those checkpoints was removed by 2005.

In recent years, with the United Kingdom's departure from the European Union, there has been some discussion of ending the Common Travel Area that encompasses the United Kingdom (including Northern Ireland), Ireland, the Isle of Man, and the Channel Islands. However, that had not taken place as of early 2018.

Northern Ireland and Industrialization

Physically, the Irish border was drawn in such a way as to trace the edges of the four counties in Northern Ireland. But how did these four counties (and the remaining two counties of Northern Ireland that don't touch the physical border) become part of Northern Ireland? Much of that answer hinges on the north's relatively high Protestant population and stronger regional support of British rule. However, there is an economic component to it, as well. Those six counties were more industrialized than the agricultural counties in the south of Ireland, thanks to the establishment of the Plantation of Ulster in the north in the first decade of the seventeenth century. The region, as a result, relied heavily on trade with Britain.

This was particularly true in Belfast, the capital of Northern Ireland, which, around the time of partition, was a fairly industrialized city and had the potential to be an important shipping port. Belfast was also a profitable center of several other industries, including linen-making, tobacco processing, rope-making, heavy engineering, and shipbuilding. Shipbuilding giant Harland and Wolff was located in Belfast and

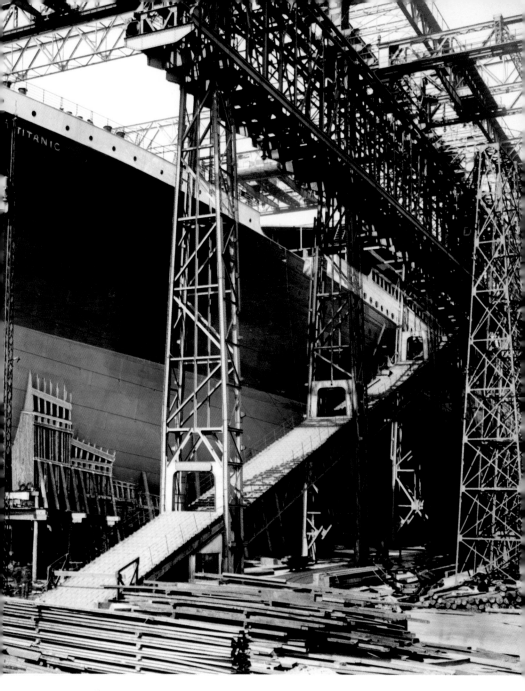

Belfast, now in Northern Ireland, was an important city in shipbuilding. The infamous *Titanic* was built in the Harland and Wolff shipyard.

THE *TITANIC* IN BELFAST

The ill-fated *Titanic* was built in Belfast by the Harland and Wolff shipyard. The building and outfitting were finished in March 1912, less than two weeks before its maiden voyage on April 10, 1912. Four days later, it would hit an iceberg in the North Atlantic and sink, killing more than fifteen hundred passengers, including the ship's architect, Thomas Andrews.

employed roughly thirty thousand people, as the largest shipbuilder in the world.

King James I granted a Charter of Incorporation to Belfast in 1613, with a couple of aims. First, he wanted to establish a new borough because each borough came with two seats in Parliament and he wanted to fill that legislative body with Protestants from the north. James's other aim was to establish Belfast as a major shipping port. A new port meant more income for the English government since it could levy customs and fees on vessels that passed through.

The problem was that the channel that led to Belfast was muddy and silty, which meant that large ships couldn't dock in Belfast—they had to drop anchor further up the channel and transport their cargo to the dock via smaller vessels.

In the early nineteenth century, Irish contractor William Dargan cut through the River Lagan and created a more usable outlet to the sea. This manmade channel was named the Victoria Channel, in honor of Queen Victoria, and helped to make Belfast an incredibly prosperous city during and after the Industrial Revolution.

Needless to say, in the late nineteenth and early twentieth centuries, when Home Rule was on everyone's mind and citizens of Ireland were strongly divided on republicanism versus unionism, the people of Northern Ireland who benefited from the prosperity of Belfast and surrounding areas were keen to remain a part of the United Kingdom. They were mostly Protestants and had experienced relative prosperity compared to the Catholics in the south, so they didn't see much need for change.

This isn't to say there wasn't industry in the southern part of Ireland. The Guinness Brewery, located in Dublin, was (and still is) a highly successful business at the time of partition. There are numerous port cities along the eastern edge of the Republic of Ireland, as well as a few along the southern coast. Mills, too, dotted all of Ireland. Still, by and large, the south tended to be more agricultural, whereas the northern areas—particularly around the Plantation of Ulster, which ultimately formed the counties of Ulster— tended to be more industrialized.

Because of the northern region's shared history, established by such geographical factors as the drumlin belt and reinforced over time by economic and cultural differences with the south, the division of the province of Ulster during partition proved to be particularly difficult. Ulster is made up of nine counties, but only six of them became part of Northern Ireland. The other

The city of Belfast was an important center in the linen industry.

three—Donegal, Cavan, and Monaghan—became part of the Republic of Ireland instead.

At the time of partition, it was largely Protestants who wanted to remain part of the United Kingdom; Catholics generally tended toward nationalism. County Donegal was—and is—largely made up of Roman Catholics, although it also has a significant minority of Protestants. The Protestants in County Donegal, though, were unique: like Catholics, they tended to be more nationalist. Counties Cavan and Monaghan had significant nationalist populations, as well. In the end, Prime Minister David Lloyd George, under whose leadership the Government of Ireland Act 1920 was drawn up, could not guarantee a unionist majority if all nine counties of Ulster were included in Northern Ireland, so it was decided that Cavan, Monaghan, and Donegal would join the Republic of Ireland.

CHAPTER FOUR
Home Rule, Nationalism, and the Partition of Ireland

T he road to the 1921 partition begins with the rise, in the 1700s, of Irish nationalism.

With the Declaratory Act of 1720, England increased its power yet again by asserting its right to pass laws that were binding on Ireland, even without the agreement of Irish Parliament. In response, Irish nationalists grew more vocal about their belief that Ireland should be self-governed. Writers such as William Molyneux and Jonathan Swift (famed for writing *A Modest Proposal* and *Gulliver's Travels*) expounded on the detrimental effects of English rule over Ireland. They found a model for the politics they were espousing—all the way across the Atlantic Ocean.

Opposite: The Battle of Dublin in 1922 marked the beginning of the Irish civil war. Armed Irish Republican Army rebels took to the streets during the battle.

Revolution and Religious Freedoms

The American Revolutionary War was all about fighting for independence from the British—a dispute to which many of the Irish could relate. On the other hand, when France and Spain declared allegiance to the United States of America, it meant that England—and by extension, Ireland—was (directly or indirectly) under attack, so many Irish people felt it important to declare their loyalty to England. In exchange, England relaxed restrictions on Ireland, allowing many Catholics the right to bear arms and easing impediments to trade. Soon, the Irish began to recognize the opportunity at hand: with England desperate to retain their loyalty, they might be able to enact reform.

In 1782, the Irish scored a major victory when their parliament was granted legislative independence from the English Parliament. What's more, later that year, the British government passed the Renunciation Act, which curtailed England's ability to enact laws on behalf of Ireland without consent.

The government also began appointing some Irish citizens to Parliament, whereas before all seats had been held by English representatives. Nevertheless, Protestants still held all the legislative seats, so Irish Catholics felt further reform was in order.

Just a few short years after the Revolutionary War ended with the United States' independence from Britain, the French Revolution broke out. This revolution also inspired Irish nationalists, who

Jonathan Swift, author of such books as *Gulliver's Travels*, skewered the idea of English rule in his writings about Ireland.

watched with interest and soon realized that the division between Protestants and Catholics was the key contributor to Ireland's lack of independence and power. If the religions could learn to coexist and co-rule, with everyone seen as Irishmen above all, then perhaps real change could occur. Reformists from the Protestant and Catholic faiths joined together to form the Society of United Irishmen.

England tried to head off Irish revolt by granting the Irish further powers, including restoring them rights of which they had long ago been stripped. In 1792 and 1793, William Pitt, the Younger, the British prime minister, passed relief acts that gave Catholics the right to vote, hold government jobs, sit on the judicial bench, and serve in the army. However, the momentum stalled there. The government eyed Irish nationalists with suspicion, having seen the revolution in America and the brewing revolution in France, and it wasn't long before the army attempted to disband the Society of United Irishmen, greatly reducing its numbers.

The society had been stripped of much of its power in Ulster, which further cemented the north as loyal to the Crown. As the years passed, it was becoming increasingly clear that Ulster was unlikely to renounce its allegiance to England.

Growing Rights for Catholics

Catholics and revolutionaries were gaining strength, and Pitt feared that England might lose its hold over

Ireland, so he set about encouraging the English and Irish parliaments to pass the Acts of Union. Pitt's first attempt failed when the Irish Parliament voted against the acts in 1799. However, the acts passed the following year and took effect in 1800.

How did the acts pass, just one year after being voted down? In a word, bribery. It's reported that members of the Irish Parliament were offered titles and honors in exchange for their votes.

The Acts of Union merged the two countries into the United Kingdom of Great Britain and Ireland, which included England, Scotland, Wales, and Ireland. They effectively dissolved the Irish Parliament and brought the country under the complete control of England and its legislature. The acts also established the United Church of England and Ireland as the official church of both nations, merged the Irish army into the British army, and established free trade between the two countries. Most appealing of all to Catholics, Pitt had promised that the Acts of Union would result in Catholic emancipation, nullifying many of the restrictions and penalties Catholics faced. The emancipation was temporarily blocked by King George III and didn't officially take effect until 1829.

In the end, Catholics in Ireland didn't see the progress they had hoped for from the Acts of Union. They still lacked key rights; for example, they could not hold a seat in Parliament. However, the law didn't state that a Catholic could not be a *candidate* for a seat in Parliament. This loophole was exploited in 1829, when Irish Catholic lawyer Daniel O'Connell won a parliamentary seat by a considerable margin.

The English Parliament's answer to O'Donnell's triumph was the Roman Catholic Relief Act 1829. Legislators across the Irish Sea were trying to stave off a revolt in the wake of increasing Catholic power. The law repealed a number of restrictions and penal laws against Catholics in Ireland and finally allowed Catholics to serve in Parliament.

It wasn't a total win for Catholics in Ireland, however. The government also enacted a fivefold increase on the fee for voting. Irish Catholics tended not to be particularly wealthy, so many could no longer afford to vote. In the end, it was a loss for Catholic voters.

The 1848 Rebellion

Under O'Connell's influence, citizens of Ireland interested in repealing the Acts of Union and reestablishing Ireland as its own nation, began to unite and rebel. However, there was division among their ranks. O'Connell believed that violence was never the answer, but others in the movement disagreed. Eventually, there was a split among Irish nationalists, with the Young Irelanders forming a separate movement that refused to rule out the use of force as a means of liberating Ireland.

In 1848, revolutions were spreading across Europe, and Ireland was no exception. Pacifist O'Connell had died in 1847, so the prominent rebels in Ireland tended

Daniel O'Connell is known as "the Liberator" in Ireland for his work on behalf of Catholics and his efforts to repeal the Acts of Union. Today, many main streets in Irish cities and towns—including Dublin, Limerick, Ennis, and Sligo—are named after O'Connell.

During the 1848 rebellion, the Irish attacked police in County Tipperary, but their efforts were quickly extinguished.

to associate with the Young Irelanders, who grew more and more willing to entertain the idea of bloodshed in the name of the cause. An uprising was planned for July 29, 1848, in South Tipperary, but when the government got wind of these plans, it arrested several key figures and the rebellion was quickly squelched.

It wasn't for nothing, however. While not everyone sanctioned violence, the Young Irelander Rebellion reestablished the idea that violence and force might be necessary to achieve the rebels' goals and free Ireland from British rule.

The Home Rule Movement

After centuries of back-and-forth over which religion should dominate in Ireland and who should rule, the final push leading to the partition of the country was the Home Rule movement.

It began when Protestant attorney Isaac Butt founded the Home Government Association in 1870. Butt's interest in the movement was largely inspired by what he saw during the Great Famine in Ireland, which took place from 1845 to 1852. During these years, the population of Ireland fell by 20–25 percent, the result of both death and emigration. The Irish had been largely dependent on potato farming for their existence, so when a potato blight wiped out their crops during the 1840s, many people starved. Disease tore through the population, too, as Irish citizens turned to

The Great Famine resulted in starvation, disease, and homelessness for many Irish citizens.

overcrowded workhouses and living accommodations in an effort to survive. People fled Ireland in droves, trying to escape the famine and disease that were ravaging the country.

During this period, the English government had a laissez-faire economic policy according to which it shouldn't help the Irish people in this time of need, since they ought to be self-sufficient by whatever means necessary. Butt saw how this policy devastated Irish families, and he felt that the Irish would be better served by becoming independent and self-governing.

The First and Second Home Rule Bills

The first Home Rule Bill was introduced in 1886 by British prime minister William Gladstone. The bill failed in the House of Commons for a number of reasons. Many legislators—both in the Conservative Party and in the Liberal Unionist Party—felt that allowing Ireland to self-govern would be the first step toward the complete disintegration of the United Kingdom of Great Britain and Ireland. Protestants in Ireland worried that Catholics, as the country's religious majority, would end up dominating Parliament and enacting pro-Catholic laws. Protestant landowners worried that such a parliament would reverse the regulations that had given them the upper hand when it came to property ownership.

In the northeastern corner of the nation, the province of Ulster was particularly opposed to Home Rule. Inhabitants of this Protestant outpost had prospered under the English and therefore had little desire to part ways with Great Britain. The pro–Great Britain Unionist Party was formed in Ulster and was joined in its cause by members of the Conservative Party.

The dream of Irish autonomy didn't die with the first Home Rule Bill. It lay quietly while England underwent governmental party changes, then resurfaced in 1893, once Gladstone had returned to power in England. Once again, the bill was defeated. However, this time, it passed in the House of Commons before it was defeated in the House of Lords. The House of Lords had broad powers to veto legislation at that time and was dominated by the Conservative Party, so there was little chance for the bill to pass.

The Third Home Rule Bill

The early twentieth century saw a cultural renaissance in Ireland. Citizens and organizations, seeing Gaelic culture slipping away, made renewed efforts to revive and cultivate the traditions from centuries past. This led to a renewed spirit of nationalism among many Irish citizens.

The passage of the Parliament Act 1911 opened the door for Home Rule once again. The Parliament Act limited the House of Lords' veto power over legislation, which meant that if the Liberal Party could get a Home Rule Bill passed in the House of Commons, the House of Lords could no longer veto it.

So, in 1912, a third Home Rule Bill was introduced. The bill would allow an Irish Parliament with limited powers to govern in such spheres as health and education. The English Parliament would still have jurisdiction when it came to security, trade, and taxation.

Unionists in the industrialized north were not in favor of the bill. Much of the southern part of the country was dominated by agriculture, and residents of Ulster felt that if citizens from those regions ruled over Ireland, they wouldn't take northern priorities into account.

Under the direction of party leaders Sir Edward Carson and James Craig, unionists in the north began to organize. They formed a provisional government in Ulster that would take power if the Home Rule Bill was passed. They also formed a private army, the Ulster Volunteer Force, in case they needed to fight to retain their citizenship in the United Kingdom of Great Britain and Ireland.

Nationalists and Home Rule Party leadership at first dismissed the unionists, skeptical that they would stand by their plan to fight. However, Carson was determined, as were those backing him, so he sought the permanent exclusion of six of the nine counties in Ulster from Home Rule. (Three of these counties had large Catholic populations, so Carson knew they were likely to side with the nationalists.)

Nationalists responded by forming their own militant force, the Irish Volunteers. They were joined by the Irish Republican Brotherhood, and for a while it seemed as if Ireland was on the brink of civil war.

The Home Rule Act passed in 1914, but it was not implemented for several years because World War I had broken out. As the United Kingdom refocused its efforts on defeating Germany, the brewing civil war in Ireland was averted. That's not to say tensions didn't still exist, but during the war, the tense topic of Home Rule was—for the most part—sidelined.

The Easter Rising and the Growth of Nationalism

Even with so many efforts concentrated on winning World War I, Irish citizens remained frustrated with English rule, and during Easter week in 1916, Irish nationalists staged a six-day uprising, taking over important locations in Dublin with the goal of establishing an independent Irish republic. The Easter Rising was an important turning point because it was the first armed action of the Irish revolutionary period, and it was the most significant Irish uprising in more than a century.

A council made up of seven members of the Irish Republican Brotherhood organized the uprising and was joined by members of the Irish Volunteers and the Irish Citizen Army. Women joined in, as well: two hundred members of the Cumann na mBan—an all-female paramilitary organization and auxiliary of the Irish Volunteers—fought alongside men.

The Irish Citizen Army was led by James Connolly, who would become a key figure in the history of the

Irish riots that followed the Easter Rising resulted in British police firing on protestors.

Home Rule movement. Connolly was born in Scotland in 1868, but his parents were Irish and the family lived in a predominantly Irish area of Edinburgh. When he was fourteen, Connolly enlisted in the British army and served in Ireland, during which time he became increasingly disillusioned with the military. He deserted the army in late 1889 or early 1890, when he learned his regiment was to continue its service in India. He married and started a family, settling in Edinburgh and joining the Scottish Socialist Federation.

Connolly was politically active wherever he went. In 1896, he and his family moved to Dublin so he could serve as secretary of the Dublin Socialist Club. Under Connolly's influence, the organization became the Irish Socialist Republican Party, which figured heavily in Ireland's move toward republicanism. In 1903, Connolly moved to the United States, where he formed the Irish Socialist Federation. He returned to Ireland in 1910 and continued his work with socialist parties, founding the Irish Citizen Army three years later.

Connolly wasn't interested in becoming involved in the Irish Volunteers, despite the fact that he was working toward similar goals. He didn't feel the organization was decisive enough when it came to matters of Irish independence. However, when the Irish Volunteers and Irish Republican Brotherhood learned that Connolly was planning an uprising against the British Empire, they approached him in the hopes of working together. At this meeting, they agreed upon Easter week as the decisive moment. As commandant of the Dublin Brigade, Connolly acted as commander in chief of the rebellion.

The six-day Easter Rising took place at numerous locations in Ireland. There were street fights in Dublin and attacks on the Royal Irish Constabulary (which had joined forces with the British) at Ashbourne, County Meath, County Cork, and County Galway. In County Wexford, the town of Enniscorthy was seized.

Nearly 500 people were killed in the uprising, more than half of whom were civilians. A third of those killed were British military and police, and only 16 percent were Irish rebels. More than 2,600 people were wounded, and parts of Dublin lay in ruin.

The British army brought in artillery, a gunboat, and thousands in reinforcements, ultimately gaining control over participants in the uprising. Patrick Pearse, a member of the Irish Republican Brotherhood and a leader in the rebellion, surrendered on April 29, 1916. At that time, the British arrested approximately 3,500 people, many of whom had not actually participated in the uprising. An estimated 1,800 prisoners— participants and bystanders alike—were sent to prisons and internment camps.

Fifteen leaders of the Easter Rising, including Connolly and Pearse, were executed. However, the Easter Rising had succeeded in at least one respect: it had shown that the Irish republicans were not afraid to use physical force to attain Ireland's independence.

The British army committed its own share of violent acts during the six-day rebellion. One activist, Francis Sheehy Skeffington, a pacifist who did not participate in the bloodshed, was arrested by the British while he was attempting to prevent looting in Dublin. Skeffington told the British officers that, although he didn't approve of their methods, he was sympathetic to the Irish nationalists' cause. The next morning, he was executed by a British firing squad. The same group of soldiers also shot and killed a young boy.

Another British regiment in Dublin spent a night during the uprising carrying out what came to be known as the North King Street Massacre. The soldiers killed fifteen male civilians in their homes, then robbed them and buried them in their backyards and cellars. Members of the regiment later claimed that they had been under orders not to take any prisoners, which they had interpreted to mean that they should shoot any suspected rebel on sight. In the end, the regiment was not held responsible for the deaths of those fifteen civilians, which inflamed the Irish.

After the Easter Rising, it seemed clear that the Home Rule Bill, in which England retained some legislative powers over Ireland, would no longer suffice. The British had violently squashed the uprising and placed thousands of Irish citizens in internment camps. This turned the tide of Irish public opinion. Many began to sympathize with the rebels and believe that the best interests of Irish citizens would only be served if Ireland declared its independence from the rest of the United Kingdom.

Sinn Féin Gains Power

After the Easter Rising, the Home Rule Party was still trying to gain public support, but the Irish citizenry was increasingly in favor of the approach set forth by Sinn Féin. The British government recognized this

One participant in the Easter Rising was Éamon de Valera. De Valera was an American citizen born to an Irish mother. His father died when he was just three years old, so de Valera was sent back to Ireland to be raised by his grandmother. In 1913, he joined the Irish Volunteers in support of Home Rule and was later a commander in the Easter Rising.

As a high-level member of the uprising, de Valera was sentenced to death. However, his sentence was commuted to life in prison because he was born an American citizen. He ended up serving only a short time and was released in 1917.

Upon his release, de Valera was elected to the House of Commons as a member of the nationalist Sinn Féin party. The president of Sinn Féin at that time should have been Irish politician Arthur Griffith, the party's founder. But Griffith, a polarizing figure, had stepped aside, allowing de Valera to take the position in the interest of creating a unified movement.

The strategy worked. Shortly after becoming the president of Sinn Féin, de Valera also took a leadership position in the Irish Volunteers. Sinn Féin hadn't participated directly in the Easter

Éamon de Valera speaks to a crowd in 1925.

Rising—that was planned and executed by other nationalist groups—but the British government was nonetheless suspicious of the party. This made it more popular among nationalists, and ultimately, under de Valera's leadership, Sinn Féin joined forces with other revolutionary groups who were interested in Irish independence. This collaboration strengthened the movement for Irish independence.

In January 1919, Sinn Féin convened an Irish Parliament, unilaterally declared an independent republic, and elected de Valera "president" of that republic. However, disputes over Ireland's independence weren't resolved there. When the Government of Ireland Act 1920 was passed, Irish nationalists in de Valera's camp were furious at its provision drawing a border through Ireland, effectively splitting the island in two. De Valera declared that the legislation fostered "political and religious rancour, which would divide Ireland into antagonistic parts." He would later refuse to support the Anglo-Irish Treaty (December 1921), even though the Irish Parliament had ratified it, because he felt that it again fell short of affirming a completely sovereign republic.

In 1926, de Valera split off from Sinn Féin to form Fianna Fáil, which billed itself as the anti-partitionist and anti-treaty party, and called partition a "crime" that had created an "unnatural boundary." While Fianna Fáil–led governments would implement key reforms, undo constitutional links with Britain, and even propose a new Irish constitution in 1937, de Valera himself would admit that it consistently failed at offering up a "clear way" to bring partition to an end and unite the whole of the island as a sovereign state.

De Valera served as head of government over three different periods, for a total of nearly two decades, until he was elected president of Ireland in 1959 at the age of seventy-five. He served a total of two terms.

and held a series of meetings with nationalist and unionist leaders called the Lloyd George talks, after the talks' facilitator, David Lloyd George, soon to be the British prime minister. It was at these sessions that the partition of Ireland was first floated as a legitimate idea. However, at the time, Lloyd George led Irish nationalist politician and Home Rule advocate John Redmond to believe that the partition would be temporary. When Redmond realized that Lloyd George intended it to be a permanent solution, he denied the agreement. The damage, however, had already been done; partitioning the country and excluding the six counties of Ulster from Home Rule was now on the table.

As the Home Rule Party continued to weaken, support for Sinn Féin grew. In 1918, nationalist sentiment rose to new heights when the British government decided to impose conscription in Ireland, which would force Irish citizens into military service for the war. The Home Rule Party and Sinn Féin joined forces to protest conscription and ultimately won; the government never enforced the plan. The combination of efforts by the Home Rule Party and Sinn Féin no doubt contributed to the success of this effort, but Sinn Féin received most of the credit.

World War I ended in November 1918, and a general election was held the following month. The Home Rule Party promised to continue its campaign for self-governance, but without any specific promises as to how it would achieve this. Sinn Féin, on the other hand, vowed to establish a parliament in Dublin,

The planned reunification never took place. The Irish War of Independence broke out between the Irish Republican Army and the British, ultimately leading to the establishment of the Irish Free State—later known simply as Ireland.

Since the partition of Ireland, twenty-six of the island's thirty-two counties have formed what is now known as Ireland, with the remaining six counties (in Ulster) making up Northern Ireland, a part of the United Kingdom.

Today, Ireland is made up of twenty-six counties comprising the majority of the island, while Northern Ireland is made up of six counties, comprising most of the province of Ulster.

CHAPTER FIVE

The Aftermath of New Borders

T he Government of Ireland Act 1920 established and enacted partition in May 1921, but that wasn't the end of the discussion—far from it, in fact. The brutal Irish War of Independence raged on, as different regions and political factions remained divided on the question of independence from Britain.

Under the new legislation, both regions of the newly divided Ireland remained part of the United Kingdom of Great Britain and Ireland, operating under Home Rule with the goal of eventual reunification. In the six counties of Northern Ireland, which had a Protestant majority, the terms of the law were largely agreeable: their counties had been mostly prosperous under British rule. In the island's remaining twenty-six counties, however, a great many citizens felt it didn't go far enough—they wanted full independence.

Opposite: In this 1921 photograph, Éamon de Valera (*sitting in the large chair*) presides over the Dáil Éireann.

Riots in Dublin during the Irish War of Independence left many buildings damaged or destroyed.

The Anglo-Irish Treaty

The Irish War of Independence, also called the Anglo-Irish War, continued for seven months after the Government of Ireland Act was passed, until finally, both sides called a truce. By the time the guerrilla war came to an end, roughly two thousand lives had been lost, with many more injured. A treaty was signed in December 1921, once both sides had realized they were at a stalemate: the IRA had proved more difficult to defeat than the British had anticipated, but the rebel group's strength was wearing thin.

The treaty established the Irish Free State, which would be a self-governing dominion under the British Empire—similar to the status of Canada and Australia today. The treaty also allowed Northern Ireland the option to opt out of joining such a state—and indeed, it chose to remain part of the United Kingdom.

On the Irish side, the treaty was agreed to by representatives of the Irish Republic—Michael Collins and Arthur Griffith among them. President Éamon de Valera, however, was not present for the discussions, and the treaty was ratified without his final input.

The settlement stirred up a great deal of conflict within Sinn Féin and the IRA, whose members were divided. Some considered it a reasonable solution—the Irish Free State would be self-governing, even if they had to swear an oath of allegiance to the British Crown. Others felt the treaty wasn't a large enough step toward

Republican forces are pictured in 1922, fighting in the Battle of Dublin, which was part of the Irish civil war.

true independence. This controversy ultimately sparked the Irish civil war, which broke out in June 1922.

Conflict Continues

The Irish civil war was sparked after an election of the provisional Irish government on June 16, 1922, saw fifty-eight seats go to pro-treaty representatives and thirty-five seats to people who were opposed to the treaty. Soon after, republicans assassinated Sir Henry Wilson, a unionist member of the English Parliament. In response, Michael Collins, a republican leader who had helped negotiate the Anglo-Irish Treaty, attacked the Four Courts in Dublin, which for a few months had been occupied by anti-treaty IRA members.

The Irish civil war lasted less than a year and, like the Irish War of Independence, was primarily waged through guerrilla warfare. The conflict was bloody, claiming at least as many casualties as the war of independence, though a final death toll has never been established. Among the dead were both Collins and Arthur Griffith.

In May 1923, pro-treaty fighters emerged victorious. By 1926, Sinn Féin had split, leading to the emergence, over the next several years, of two major political parties in Ireland: Fianna Fáil and Fine Gael.

The Troubles

While conflict emerged in the Republic of Ireland right after the partition, tensions in the north took longer to boil over—several decades, in fact, until the late 1960s, when the Troubles broke out.

The Troubles comprised a guerrilla war triggered by ethno-nationalist conflict. While, by and large, Catholics did not support the partition of Ireland and the idea of Northern Ireland remaining under UK rule, the Troubles actually weren't a religious

In this photo from 1972, children throw debris at a British tank on patrol in Belfast, Northern Ireland.

conflict. Rather, they were driven by nationalist and political clashes.

Irish nationalists in Northern Ireland were mostly Catholic, but their interest in rejoining the Republic of Ireland was more about a united Ireland than about religion. In contrast, the unionists were mostly Protestant, but their interest in remaining part of the United Kingdom had more to do with the desire to be of British nationality than it did with their religion.

There was, of course, a religious component. When Northern Ireland was partitioned from the Irish Free State, its six counties had a strong Protestant and unionist majority. As a result, the Catholic minority, which tended to favor republicanism, faced discrimination. For example, gerrymandering—that is, manipulating the boundaries of an electoral area so that its votes favor a particular political party—meant that they had little voice in government. They also faced discrimination in employment and public housing.

The Northern Ireland Civil Rights Association worked to end this discrimination, but unionists denounced their work, sometimes resorting to violence. This led to the outbreak of the Troubles, which lasted for thirty years and involved many conflicts in Northern Ireland, claiming the lives of about thirty-five hundred people and injuring approximately forty-seven thousand more.

The conflict was largely fought by paramilitary groups. The IRA was on the side of republicans, along with the Irish National Liberation Army and the Irish

People's Liberation Organisation. On the side of the unionists were the Ulster Volunteer Force, the Ulster Defence Association, the Ulster Resistance, and the Red Hand Commando.

The Good Friday Agreement

After thirty years, the Troubles officially came to an end in 1998, with the signing of the Good Friday Agreement. The accord addressed the relationships between Northern Ireland and the Republic of Ireland and between the Republic of Ireland and the United Kingdom. The issues covered included civil rights, cultural rights, weapons decommissioning, policing, and sovereignty.

In short, the agreement set forth that, if or when a majority of citizens from Northern Ireland and from the Republic of Ireland vote for reunification, the British and Irish governments will implement that process. Until then, Northern Ireland will remain part of the United Kingdom. The Good Friday Agreement also brought about the repeal of the Government of Ireland Act 1920.

Because of the large minority of republicans in Northern Ireland, the agreement also allowed the people of Northern Ireland to establish their citizenship as either British or Irish. Finally, it demanded that cultural, linguistic, and social traditions be respected in the hopes of ending discrimination against those in Northern Ireland who wished to honor and retain their connection to their Irish heritage.

A POLICY OF NONVIOLENCE

The Northern Ireland Civil Rights Association was a pacifist organization that employed nonviolent protest methods to fight for the civil rights of underrepresented Catholics in Northern Ireland. They were inspired by the nonviolent resistance made famous by American civil rights leader Dr. Martin Luther King Jr.

Brexit and the Northern Ireland Question

Since the Good Friday Agreement, life in Northern Ireland has been far more peaceful. There have been minor conflicts, though nothing on the scale of what the region saw during the Troubles. However, the United Kingdom's impending withdrawal from the European Union, commonly known as Brexit (a portmanteau of "British exit"), has thrown the future of Northern Ireland into question once again.

The European Union, founded in 1993, is a confederation of the majority of countries in Europe. It has twenty-eight member nations and functions somewhat like the United States: there's a standardized system of laws that apply to all members, and people can move freely across borders within the union. Many of the states also use the union's official currency, the euro.

However, in 2016, the United Kingdom became the first member state to initiate its withdrawal from the

In March 2017, about nine months after the United Kingdom's vote to leave the European Union, people gather in Dublin to protest a hard border between Northern Ireland and the Republic of Ireland.

European Union, with 51.9 percent of British citizens voting for Brexit. Leaving the EU will take several years, with the United Kingdom on course to leave the European Union by March 2019. The exit may turn out to be what's called a "soft exit," in which the United Kingdom retains some membership benefits in the European Union, or a "hard exit," in which the UK would be wholly separate from the European Union for the purposes of trade and movement of people across borders—but how Brexit will affect the United Kingdom as a whole remains unknown.

Because Scotland voted to stay a part of the European Union, there was talk among some analysts and politicians in late 2017 that the region might vote for its own independence from England in order to return to the EU. Northern Ireland faces similar questions. In 2017, the European Parliament published a brief concluding that "Northern Ireland is the part of the UK most distinctly affected by Brexit." Nationalists in Northern Ireland also voted to remain in the European Union, winning out over the unionists who voted to leave, but their input proved inconsequential: the consent of the Northern Ireland Assembly was not constitutionally or politically necessary in order to proceed with Brexit. The 1998 Northern Ireland Act gave the Northern Ireland Assembly the right to pass laws, but not in all policy areas—and the British Parliament still has the right to make laws for Northern Ireland.

Under Brexit, Northern Ireland would, along with the rest of the country, remove itself from the European Union. However, the Republic of Ireland would still be a part of the EU. Because the Irish border is open, and because travel between member states of the European Union is also open, citizens of the European Union could, in theory, travel to the Republic of Ireland and then cross the border into Northern Ireland—thus freely entering the United Kingdom.

As of early 2018, no decision had been reached about whether to enforce border controls on the Irish border or otherwise create a "hard border" there, doing away with the existing Common Travel Area. The problem is, enforcing border controls between the two parts of Ireland would be a violation of the Good Friday Agreement, so the idea of a hard border has been met with fierce opposition, including from the former secretary of state for Northern Ireland, Peter Hain, who suggested that the United Kingdom should be responsible for offering up a solution that doesn't include a hard border. According to Hain, "A hard border would damage the economy by restricting trade, and harm the lives of thousands of people who cross it every day. And in doing so, it would damage the peace process at a time when power-sharing has never looked so fragile."

The Brexit negotiator for the European Parliament, Guy Verhofstadt, has suggested that Northern Ireland could potentially stay in the single market or customs union after Brexit, which might avoid the issue of creating a hard border. However, staunch unionists have opposed this plan because it differentiates between Northern Ireland and the rest of the United Kingdom.

If Northern Ireland reunified with Ireland, it would once again be part of the European Union. The prime minister of the Republic of Ireland, Leo Varadkar, stated in October 2017 that he suspected even unionist

The Irish border is one of the stickiest issues in Brexit. Relations between the Republic of Ireland and Northern Ireland have improved over the decades since partition, but it is still a fragile relationship. Doing away with the Common Travel Area between the two countries would have significant consequences, not just for political relations, but for trade. There are four main ways the border issue can be handled.

One solution is to enforce a hard border along the currently permeable, and in many places unmarked, Irish border. Not only would this be a strong symbol of division between the two parts of Ireland, it would also be very difficult to enforce. The Irish border runs through fields, rivers, and forests, meandering along a tortuous and complex path. It would require significant manpower to patrol such a border.

Another option is to create special status for Northern Ireland, whereupon the region could remain a part of the European Union in some capacity. The British government hasn't exhibited strong support for this option, and neither have unionists, who don't want to cause a rift between Northern Ireland and the United Kingdom.

A third option is to keep the Common Travel Area as it is, but then make the sea borders around the island hard borders, requiring passports and customs checks at airports and seaports. This option isn't popular among the North Irish, who would then have to travel as foreigners any time they went to the rest of the United Kingdom.

The fourth option is the reunification of the Republic of Ireland and Northern Ireland—but in the face of this possibility, the old divisions remain.

One of the most complicated segments of the frontier involves a small piece of land, occupied by only about a hundred people, that belongs to the Republic of Ireland but is almost completely surrounded by Northern Irish territory. Called the Drummully

The Belcoo River forms a part of the border between Northern Ireland and the Republic of Ireland.

Polyp and characterized by small hills, or drumlins, the area measures only about 7 miles (11.3 km) by 3 miles (4.8 km) at its widest. A narrow strip of land, free of roads, connects it to the south, which means that inhabitants of this territory must drive across the border and back just to visit the rest of the Republic of Ireland. This would pose a problem if such crossings became more cumbersome. In fact, the main access road to the Drummully Polyp crosses the border no less than four times over a distance of just 7 miles (11.3 km).

citizens of Northern Ireland would want to be citizens of Ireland for the purposes of convenience with regards to travel and trade.

Winners and Losers

So who are the winners and losers after partition? That's a complicated question. Some people believe that partition offered the island of Ireland the best of both worlds. Those in the north who wanted to remain part of the United Kingdom were able to do so, and those who wanted independence achieved it.

Partition, however, also came at a cost. Many nationalists ended up the minority in unionist territory, and vice versa. Thousands of people lost their lives in the conflicts leading up to partition, and the bloodshed continued for many decades after.

The split between Northern Ireland and Ireland has also obscured a common heritage. There are Northern Irish citizens who continue to honor their Irish roots, but they live in a region where Irish Gaelic is no longer one of the main languages. According to the 2011 census, only about 3.7 percent of the population of Northern Ireland could speak, read, write, and understand Gaelic. The streets signs are all in English, as are most store signs. By comparison, in Ireland, Gaelic and English are both official languages, and schoolchildren are generally taught both English and Gaelic.

Who benefited and who suffered as a result of partition is a difficult issue that can't be explained in black and white. Even once Brexit is settled and decisions are made about Northern Ireland, tensions around the border may still exist. The Emerald Isle, even after the partition that split it in two, is still experiencing that constant ebb and flow, that clash between the past and future, between settlers and the settled, that has defined it for a thousand years.

CHRONOLOGY

- **1169 CE**   The Norman Invasion begins.

- **1316**   Edward Bruce is crowned king of Ireland as Gaelic Irish attempt to regain control of Ireland.

- **1394**   King Richard II arrives in Ireland with ten thousand troops and gains control of a number of territories across Ireland.

- **1455**   The Wars of the Roses begin, with the Houses of Lancaster and York battling for control of the English monarchy.

- **1509**   Henry VIII becomes king of England.

- **1534**   The Act of Supremacy installs Henry VIII as the Supreme Head on Earth of the Church of England, effectively bringing England under Protestant rule, sparking the English Reformation, and transforming England from a Catholic country into a Protestant one.

- **1536**   The Irish Parliament establishes the Church of Ireland as the country's official religious body.

- **1541**   Henry VIII is declared king of Ireland.

- **1569**   The Desmond Rebellion begins in Munster.

- **1593**   The Nine Years' War begins with a conflict over how Irish Gaelic lord Hugh O'Neill, Earl of Tyrone, was to rule his lands in Ulster.

- **1603**   The Nine Years' War ends, leaving Ireland completely under British rule.

• **1609**	The Plantation of Ulster is established.
• **1641**	The native Irish working on the Plantation of Ulster stage the Irish Rebellion. Thousands are killed over several months of fighting.
• **1642**	The Confederation of Kilkenny, a group of Catholics charged with administering Catholic parts of the island, is established in response to the Irish Rebellion. Conflicting goals will tear it apart only seven years later.
• **1649**	Charles I is executed; Oliver Cromwell is established as a political leader and arrives in Ireland with an army of thousands.
• **1653**	Cromwell's army defeats Catholic Ireland and restores English rule.
• **1662**	King Charles II passes the Act of Settlement, which states that anyone who could prove they weren't involved in the Irish Rebellion could get their land back.
• **1688**	Protestantism has finally and definitively deposed Catholicism as the official religion of the English Crown.
• **1668**	With the Glorious Revolution, King James II of England is overthrown.
• **1689**	The War of the Three Kings breaks out, as James II enlists the help of King Louis XIV of France to battle William of Orange and his wife, Mary, for the English throne.

CHRONOLOGY

- **1691**   The Treaty of Limerick ends the War of the Three Kings.

- **1697**   Parliament passes the Banishment Act, requiring most Catholic clergy to leave Ireland.

- **1782**   The Irish Parliament is granted legislative independence from the English Parliament, and the Renunciation Act is passed, curtailing England's ability to enact laws on behalf of Ireland.

- **1800**   The Acts of Union create the United Kingdom of Great Britain and Ireland, which includes England, Scotland, Wales, and Ireland.

- **1829**   After Irish Catholic lawyer Daniel O'Connell wins a seat in the Irish Parliament, the Roman Catholic Relief Act repeals a number of anti-Catholic laws.

- **1845**   The Great Famine begins in Ireland.

- **1848**   The Young Irelander Rebellion breaks out and is quickly squelched.

- **1886**   The first Home Rule Bill is introduced in English Parliament.

- **1893**   The second Home Rule Bill is introduced in English Parliament.

- **1911**   The Parliament Act is passed, and the House of Lords can no longer veto the Home Rule bills.

- **1912**   The third Home Rule Bill is introduced in English Parliament.

- **1914**   The Home Rule Act is passed.

- **1916**   Irish nationalists stage a six-day rebellion, called the Easter Rising, with the goal of establishing an independent Irish republic.

- **1918**   Nationalist political party Sinn Féin wins the general election in Ireland.

- **1919**   Dáil Éireann, a Sinn Féin–assembled parliament, meets for the first time. The Irish War for Independence breaks out.

- **1920**   The Government of Ireland Act is passed, officially partitioning Ireland.

- **1922**   The Irish civil war breaks out over conditions of the Anglo-Irish Treaty, which ended the Irish War for Independence.

- **1998**   After thirty years of unrest and sometimes-violent conflict in Northern Ireland, the Good Friday Agreement ends the historical period known as the Troubles.

Common Travel Area An open-borders area made up of the United Kingdom, Ireland, the Isle of Man, and the Channel Islands.

conscription Forced enlistment for military service; also called a draft.

dominion A self-governing territory of the British Commonwealth.

emigration Leaving one's country to settle in another.

estuary Where the mouth of a large river meets the sea.

ethno-nationalism A form of nationalism wherein a nation is defined by different ethnicities.

excommunicate To exclude a person from participation in the Christian Church.

figurehead A leader who doesn't hold much real power.

fjord Long, narrow inlet of sea between high cliffs.

gerrymandering Manipulating the boundaries of an electoral area so that the area votes in favor of a particular political party.

guerrilla war A war in which small groups of soldiers fight against larger, regular forces.

heretic A person whose religious practices are outside the accepted norm.

House of Commons The lower house of Parliament in the United Kingdom.

House of Lords The upper house of Parliament in the United Kingdom.

laissez-faire A policy in which the government does not interfere with the workings of the free market.

linguistic Relating to language.

nationalism Advocacy for political independence of one's country.

pagan Relating to non-Christian or pre-Christian religious beliefs.

paramilitary An unofficial force that is organized similarly to a military force.

pardon Forgiveness of the legal consequences of an offense or conviction.

portmanteau A word that blends the sounds and meanings of two other words.

potato blight A fungal disease that destroyed the Irish potato crop and plunged the country into famine.

Rump Parliament Part of the Long Parliament in England that continued to sit after Presbyterian members were excluded in 1648.

sovereign state A state that administers its own government and is not dependent on another power.

undertaker In the context of Irish history, a rich man from England or Scotland who took over land seized from the Irish and settled it with other members of the Protestant faith.

writ A written command in the name of the court or another legal authority.

FURTHER INFORMATION

Books

Cochrane, Feargal. *Northern Ireland: The Reluctant Peace*. New Haven, CT: Yale University Press, 2013.

Collins, Michael. *A Path to Freedom: Articles and Speeches by Michael Collins*. Cork, Ireland: Mercier Press, 2011.

Fanning, Ronan. *Éamon de Valera: A Will to Power*. Cambridge, MA: Harvard University Press, 2016.

Killeen, Richard. *A Brief History of Ireland*. Philadelphia, PA: Running Press, 2012.

Osborne-McKnight, Juilene. *The Story We Carry in Our Bones*. Gretna, LA: Pelican Publishing, 2015.

Websites

The IRA & Sinn Féin
www.pbs.org/wgbh/pages/frontline/shows/ira/inside/org.html

This site, run by PBS, provides a comprehensive history of the IRA and Sinn Féin, with numerous links to related topics.

Irish Culture and Customs
www.irishcultureandcustoms.com

This site contains interesting information about Irish culture and customs, along with many links where readers can delve deeper.

FURTHER INFORMATION

Living in Ireland

www.livinginireland.ie

This website is designed for nonnative people living in Ireland, but it has many helpful links about the history of Ireland; its political system; and work, housing, and education policies.

Videos

Northern Ireland's Troubles: Walls of Shame

www.youtube.com/watch?v=HZM-OC0p9us

This documentary explores life in Ireland versus Northern Ireland, including the Troubles, the Good Friday Agreement, and more recent attempts at peaceful coexistence.

Soldiers' Stories: Northern Ireland

www.youtube.com/watch?v=MZULAbyfs0k

This documentary covers the three decades during which the Troubles took place.

This Is Ireland

www.youtube.com/watch?v=Rk8VibKA4Ws

This video provides a broad introduction to Irish culture, heritage, and landscape.

BBC News. "1917–20: The Road to Partition." March 18, 1999. http://news.bbc.co.uk/2/hi/events/northern_ireland/history/64204.stm.

Delaney, Frank. *Ireland: A Novel*. New York: HarperCollins Publishers, 2005.

Duncan, Pamela. "Donegal: Up Here It's Truly Different." *Irish Times*, December 29, 2012. https://www.irishtimes.com/news/donegal-up-here-it-s-truly-different-1.5481.

Haigh, Christopher, ed. *The Cambridge Historical Encyclopedia of Great Britain and Ireland*. Cambridge, MA: Cambridge University Press, 1985.

Hunt, Darren. "Ireland PM's Shock Claim Northern Irish Will Abandon UK for EU Citizenship After Brexit." *Express*, October 19, 2017. http://www.express.co.uk/news/uk/868507/Brexit-news-UK-EU-Theresa-May-latest-European-Union-Council-summit-Ireland-video.

Jackson, Alvin, ed. *The Oxford Handbook of Modern Irish History*. Oxford, UK: Oxford University Press, 2014.

Kelly, Stephen. *Fianna Fáil, Partition and Northern Ireland, 1926–1971*. Sallins, Ireland: Irish Academic Press, 2013.

Lenihan, Pádraig, ed. *Conquest and Resistance: War in Seventeenth-Century Ireland*. Leiden, Netherlands: Koninklijke Brill, 2001.

Madden, F. J. M. *The History of Ireland*. Chicago, IL: Contemporary Books, 2005.

McCreary, Alf. "The Industrial Revolution Transformed Belfast, Making It Ireland's Biggest City—and It All Began with the Port." *Belfast Telegraph Digital*, January 22, 2014. http://www.belfasttelegraph.co.uk/archive/belfast-400/the-industrial-revolution-transformed-belfast-making-it-irelands-biggest-city-and-it-all-began-with-the-port-29224161.html.

McDonald, Henry. "Northern Ireland Could Stay in Customs Union After Brexit—Verhofstadt." *Guardian*, September 20, 2017. https://www.theguardian.com/politics/2017/sep/20/northern-ireland-stay-customs-union-after-brexit-verhofstadt.

McNally, Frank. "Borderline Nationality Disorder." *Irish Times*, September 18, 2013. https://www.irishtimes.com/culture/heritage/borderline-nationality-disorder-1.1530942.

Meagher, Kevin. "An Irish Sea Border—and 3 Other Tricky Options for Northern Ireland After Brexit." *New Statesman*, July 28, 2017. https://www.newstatesman.com/politics/staggers/2017/07/irish-sea-border-and-3-other-tricky-options-northern-ireland-after-brexit.

Nash, Catherine, Bryonie Reid, and Brian Graham. *Partitioned Lives: The Irish Borderlands*. New York: Routledge, 2016.

The National Archives. "Irish Civil War: Partition and Civil War." The Cabinet Papers. Accessed December 4, 2017. http://www.nationalarchives.gov.uk/cabinetpapers/themes/irish-civil-war.htm.

Thompson, Sylvia. "Ireland's Industrial Heritage: The Past You Might Not Know We Had." *Irish Times*, August 22, 2015. https://www.irishtimes.com/culture/heritage/ireland-s-industrial-heritage-the-past-you-might-not-know-we-had-1.2324451.

Tonge, Jonathan. "The Impact and Consequences of Brexit for Northern Ireland." European Parliament, 2017. http://www.europarl.europa.eu/RegData/etudes/BRIE/2017/583116/IPOL_BRI(2017)583116_EN.pdf.

INDEX

INDEX

Cathleen Small is a writer and editor. She is the author of nearly four dozen books on a variety of topics, including history, technology, and biography. She has traveled extensively in Europe but has not yet made it to the Emerald Isle—a wrong she intends to right as soon as possible. When she's not writing or editing, Small enjoys reading and traveling with her husband and two young sons.